MW00940482

"Seems like you pa

I was looking forward to October.
The fall scents, apple cider, candy corn, and pumpkins.
Our very own pumpkin.
In February it all changed.
"Seems like you passed everything already," said the doctor
as she gave us the news that our baby didn't make it.
Within the past couple of months
I've realized that those words are untrue.
See with loss, you open the door to deep pain.
You tiptoe your way around the wound
with fear of reopening that scar.
I questioned God and His goodness.
I struggled to share because the words wouldn't come to the
surface. I found myself at such a weak place.
Some days were full of strength,
but most days, I questioned my purpose.
Loss took a piece of my heart that I won't see until heaven, but it's
also brought me to a place where I've found myself desperately
clinging to God, and striving to live slowly.
Relishing the moments and the people around me.
That doesn't mean I'm no longer hurting,
nor does it mean that I'm okay.
I don't know if I'll ever be "okay" with the loss I've experienced,
but I do know that through the short months
of our first child growing inside of me,
that baby, our angel baby has changed my life
and birthed something beautiful.

the mourning sister

A JOURNEY OF GRIEF AND JOY

JOSEFINA HERRERA SANDERS

for

Our sweet Baby Sanders resting in heaven.

I wish we could've met, but God had bigger plans.
You have changed me and dada's life forever.

This book is also for those who have experienced loss and
are currently navigating through a new season of life.
I see you, I hear you, I am you.

This is for you. This is for us.

Forward

Loss is something that will touch each of our souls at one point or another. Intertwined in what escapes us can also extend a lesson of some sort, even when our hearts are too tender to see it. The Mourning Sister is a collection of, not only life lessons encouraged by a devastating loss, but also affirmations and self-love notes that serve as salve for a healing soul. Being a woman who's had a miscarriage, this collection of work brought tears to my eyes, warmth to my body from the relatable words that created a welcoming embrace, and it showed me the importance of camaraderie. Standing together in sisterhood as we move through our respective losses and healing work is what The Mourning Sister brings to the world.

Josefina's vulnerability, honesty, and bravery speak volumes through these pages. I hope that you're able to nestle into this book with a sense of comfort and community.

We are not alone in this life as we grieve, mend, and unfold.

In Sisterhood,
Alexandra Elle

ferial

to the one with empty arms

you're still a mother.
you're still a fighter.
you're still beautiful.

take your time nurturing your soul.

your empty arms
don't make you deficient.

you alone,
are loved,
seen,
and remembered.

to the childless without a choice

out of the rib you've been created and
since the beginning you've been needed.

take your time nurturing your soul.

whatever you're lacking
doesn't make you incomplete.

you alone,
are loved,
seen,
and remembered.

to the motherless and hurting

the void you feel is acknowledged,
and understood,
you're still a daughter and nothing less.

take your time nurturing your soul.

despite being motherless that
doesn't mean you're lacking.

you alone,
are loved,
seen,
and remembered.

grief

has

no

color.

reflections

my struggle is my strength, and my body is still beautiful.
my struggle is my strength, and my body is still beautiful.
my struggle is my strength, and my body is still beautiful.
my struggle is my strength, and my body is still beautiful.
my struggle is my strength, and my body is still beautiful.
my struggle is my strength, and my body is still beautiful.
my struggle is my strength, and my body is still beautiful.
my struggle is my strength, and my body is still beautiful.

no sense, nonsense

it doesn't make sense.
one life losing another life,
yet i'm still breathing.

passing "everything" already
yet, i'm still feeling.

all the signs of death,
yet i'm still believing.

that my baby isn't leaving.

i didn't know that you can feel pregnant
with no life inside of you.
i didn't know that though a life ended,
your body keeps continues moving.
when the baby left my body,
there were still pieces in me
that believed it wasn't

d e n i a l.

you are part of this process.
not just within my body,
but also within my soul.

sometimes we carry things
without realizing
they are already gone.

flowers don't bloom all year.
but you will surely bloom.

note to self

loss isn't a breeze.
it isn't something that you are prepared for.
in fact it's something you avoid thinking of.
no amount of prayer can keep you from feeling the pain.
no amount of busyness, can keep you from facing pain.

your brain cannot understand what just happened.
your soul doesn't want to.
this part of the journey is needed too.

take your time grieving.
make it a point to write those emotions.
listen to your body and heart's desire.
don't hesitate to pause and pray.
your soul needs replenishing,
and your heart needs encouragement.

don't be afraid to make selfish decisions
as you face one of the hardest moments in life.

in this season, you are still strong even as you are weak.

God is our refuge and strength a very present help in trouble.

PSALM 46:1

It was during this time where I questioned God's goodness in my life. If He loved me, why would He allow my body to fail me? If He loved me, why would He let bad things happen to good people? Why would he allow grief to be part of someone's journey?

I fist-fought denial hard. I didn't want to believe that my body rejected life. I couldn't believe that my womb failed to hold on to the product of love that was forming within. I was hurting, badly. At the time I didn't think that anything good would come out of this. There were days that I rubbed my lifeless womb, in hopes of revitalizing the love that dwelled inside of it.

This part of the grieving process is part of it. It was also the beginning of the journey to self-love, self-discovery, and self-care.

While it was painful, it was also growing.

Writing is healing. Use this space to journal your journey.

anger

process

anger is part of the process
touch it,
feel it,
and let it go.

still

i want to celebrate
her rainbow.
at the same time,
i want to cry.

please don't

don't tell me it wasn't God's timing.
do not try to cover my wound.
don't make promises for my body.
pity is not allowed in this room.

possess

it's okay to feel anger.
it's okay to question.
it's okay to set boundaries to avoid triggers.

my emotions are real,
but they do not control me.

my emotions are legitimate,
but they do not possess me.

my emotions are valid,
but they do not own me.

invitation

"welcome to the club"
i fully embraced the invitation.

welcome to "the club"

the same words that brought melodies to my life,
pierced me right where it hurts most,
my heart.

i don't want to enter through the doors of loss.

i am angry at my body,
angry because it let me down.

at the same time
i'm depending on it
because it's holding me up.

freedom

today i release you

in order to move forward
i must unclench my fists.

receive

i'm releasing guilt
and receiving grace.
i'm releasing hurt
and receiving healing.
i'm releasing anger
and receiving acceptance.

making space for healing by:

- setting unapologetic boundaries
- logging off and staying off
- allowing myself to release my emotions
- decluttering physically, mentally,
emotionally, and spiritually
- eating better
- saying no to things that may trigger me
- journaling my grief
- using a punching bag
- saying no

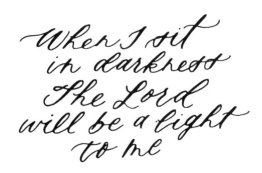

When I sit
in darkness
The Lord
will be a light
to me

MICAH 7:8

When we first learned about our miscarriage, it was very traumatic. The doctor was cold, and it seemed like she didn't care. In that moment, I was feeling so many emotions, but anger wasn't one of them. I'd be lying if I said that things remained that way.

As I began to face my trauma, I became angry.

Angry at God, mad at those around me who were growing little lives, and, furious with myself.

I blamed myself for the tragedy.

For not being able to fix things, and for overworking myself. My anger built through guilt, and I couldn't breakthrough without facing the reality that sometimes bad things, just happen. As I walked through the anger in my grief, I found freedom. Not because I suppressed my emotions, or put a bandage of scripture, but because I faced it head on and shed truth and light to the darkness, the guilt, and the lies that tried to consume me.

When I confronted my anger, I found freedom.

Writing is freeing. Use this space to journal your journey.

bargaining

sacred dancing

some days i'm dancing with hope.
some days i'm dancing with anger.
and so, i'm still dancing.

twists and turns,
still I keep dancing.

growth

the only way to grow through it
is by walking through it.

words to my husband

we started with hope
and because of hurt, i've turned away.
as much as this pain divides us
i'm here to stay.

here's to holding and hoping.

grieving and still

i am grieving loss, but i am still living.
i am grieving disappointment, but i am still hopeful.

i am grieving the failure of my body,
but i am still enjoying it's purpose.

i am grieving timeline,
but i am still enjoying the journey.

up

you can't just erase the painful memories.
you can't change the outcome.
nothing and no one can
change the way that you feel.
they can't stop the wave of emotions
that rush into you.
they can't keep you from falling.

but the thing about falling,
and finding yourself in such a low estate is,
all you can do is look up.

for a friend

you can ask me about my experience
without tip-toeing around it.
you can tell me that you love me
without saying anything.
you can share about pain
without measuring mine.
you can tell me you don't understand
without giving me a reason why.

we grieve.
we hurt.
we may even lose ourselves in the process.

but, we will heal.
we will bloom.
we will be okay.

we just need you to hold our hand while we're walking.

you

don't

have

to

rush

the

process.

p a c e

yourself.

Affirmations

i can be joyful in the midst of my grief.
i will be gentle in the midst of my grief.
i can be joyful in the midst of my grief.
i will be gentle in the midst of my grief.
i can be joyful in the midst of my grief.
i will be gentle in the midst of my grief.
i can be joyful in the midst of my grief.
i will be gentle in the midst of my grief.
i can be joyful in the midst of my grief.
i will be gentle in the midst of my grief.

a season of

breaking and becoming

neglecting and nurturing

loving and losing

growing and going

*a time to weep
and a time to laugh,
a time to mourn
and a time to dance.*

ECCLESIASTES 3:4

There was a point in my grief where I laughed to the point of
tears. I felt guilty for laughing during loss.
I felt ashamed for expressing such joy
during one of the hardest moments of my life.
I remember after that moment, rushing myself to get pregnant.
I wanted to feel joy, I wanted to dance without guilt,
I wanted to laugh without thinking of the loss.
Month after month of trying to conceive,
I grew weary, my body did too.
I was doing too much.
Then I read this verse,
a time to weep and a time to laugh,
a time to mourn and a time to dance.
As I read these powerful words I realized the beauty in duality.
I realized that we have permission to do both.
I can dance with joy and dance with grief,
at the same time.

Writing is illuminating. Use this space to journal your journey.

depression

garden

let those tears fall,
they'll help the garden grow

oblivion

there was a point in my life
where numbness was the solution to my pain.
i tried filling the void of emptiness and insecurity
with anything that kept me distracted.
i ran away from sobriety
and kept myself far away
from facing my wounds.

life seemed so much better in oblivion.

mirror

before i lost you,
i already lost myself

you just had a way
of revealing to me

what i hid from.

body changes

they never really told me
how different things would be
what once filled me up with life
now seems incomplete.

rainbows

note to self:
don't give up.
your rainbow

will soon come.

the waiting

it seems like the longer the wait,
the deeper the pain.

as the baby announcements show up,
the doubt of never becoming what I desire
takes up all the space.

in my mind and in my heart
discouragement is all that i feel.

i just want to rush this process.
i just want to heal.

the sadness is also part of the process
weep, pray, yell, scream,
honor your emotions.
talk to God about it.
don't hold on to hurt,
and don't rest in it.

inhale the journey
exhale expectation.

grief has no timeline.

it is imperfect and unpretty.

i can be okay one moment,
and hurt the next.

but, i will be gentle with myself,
as i learn to live with loss.

lavender

the calm
and sweetness of
life you gave to me

when i carried my babe,
all i wanted was lavender.

Why, my soul, are you downcast?
Why so disturbed within me?
Put your hope in God,
for I will yet praise him,
My Savior My God.

PSALM 42:11

When I was younger,
I resorted to all kinds of things to distract me from hurt.
At eighteen years old, I remember being on the hospital bed
getting my stomach pumped out because I tried to take my life.
Depression is something that I've always struggled with.
I've watched people I love fight this mental illness,
and it wasn't until our miscarriage that I realized my mental
illness came from a hormonal disorder.
During this season,
I've learned to observe, prepare, and face my depression.
Some days I fight back, other days, I soak in it.
I've learned that self-care plays a huge role in mending my pain.
I take the day off, I allow myself to cry, I read, I pray, meditate,
receive therapy, and most importantly,
I practice the art of gratitude.

Writing is rejuvenating. Use this space to journal your journey.

acceptance

waves

grief comes in waves.
sometimes it looks like sleeping all day.
other times it's full of distractions
to keep you at arm's length from hurt.
but every grieving phase is necessary for true healing.

purpose

in you,
i found love.
because of you,
i've experienced love.
through you,
I know i'm loved.

today i choose to live loved.

uncover

as i uncover my wounds
and let them lay bare
i find myself,
slowly healing.

letting go

i'm letting you go
and holding you close.
remembering your life,
with hopes to never forget
the life you gave to me.

waiting room

i know that she is coming.
as i wait for these double lines,
i'll praise God in the waiting room.

while this journey has been bitter,
it has led me to something sweet.

joy.

i finally understand that i can be joyful
in the midst of mourning.

in power

i am beautiful.
i am strong.
i am capable to do all things.
i can be broken yet, still be beautiful.
my story matters.
my life matters.

balance

it's okay
to move forward
and mourn
at the same time.

for the mourning sister

as you walk this journey,
remember that you can go at your pace.
you can walk through a similar loss,
but we do not grieve the same.

you are not alone in your grief.
there are many of us here.
so as you navigate these waters,
hold on and do not fear.

treasure the sweet memories,
and get rid of expectation.
you will get through this.
seek community and self-preservation.

permission

i give myself permission to laugh.
to hope.
to try again.

i will fight fear.
and embrace freedom.

gratitude

i am grateful for my body.
i am grateful for my support.
i am grateful for new friendships.
i am grateful for this season,
i am grateful for the growth.

i have so many reasons to give praise.

to my body

you are not broken,
you are whole.
you are not incomplete,
you are enough.
you are not undeserving,
you are worthy.

you are not incurable,
you will heal.

you are resilient.
you are allowed to love.
you will produce love.

purpose

one morning i woke up, and told myself
it's time to deal with this.

i showered, ate, and put on some clothes.
i took the keys and got in the car.

two minutes in, while driving into the main road,
my heart began beating quickly.
i felt as if i couldn't breathe.
the flashbacks of pain and blood were all I could see.
i quickly turned the car back around, and sped home.

i couldn't do it.
my broken heart was overwhelmed.

what use to look so endearing to me,
somehow felt unbearable.
the world was too big, and i felt so small,
so fragile, and so broken.

i ran inside my house and cried.
as i wept and tried to keep composure
i felt something suddenly i hadn't felt in a while,
my heartbeat.

for I have learned
to be content
whatever the circumstances.

PHILIPPIANS 4:11

Each and everyone of us walk around with an imaginary
wristband stamped with fear.

Fear of failure. Fear or not measuring up. Fear of loss.

Fear of losing again. Fear of _____.

But what if we reach that?

What if that fear of ours comes to life?

What happens next?

Life. Life continues, and so do we.

You move forward, with a scar.

As I continue moving forward in this journey of life,
it doesn't mean I plan on forgetting.

But it does mean choosing to remember.

Remember what?

Remembering to choose joy over fear and pain.

Remembering to allow myself to enjoy the journey.

Remembering to be gentle to myself.

Remembering that as we walk this road of life, and heal
during the toughest losses, I am to be fully present.

Writing is renewing. Use this space to journal your journey.

_____

_____

_____

_____

_____

_____

_____

_____

_____

_____

_____

_____

_____

_____

_____

_____

_____

use the following pages to write some more.
here are some journal questions you can answer?

how are you feeling?
what are you grateful for?
what are you inhaling and exhaling?
who are you angry at and why?
how can you be gentle to yourself during the days
you feel guilt?
what does it look like to let go and hold near?

Thank you so much for taking the time to journey with me,
and for allowing me to share my grief with you.

If you find your heart heavy at this moment,
take the time to nurture it.
Sit in with those emotions, and write out your feelings.

That's exactly what I did with every piece you find in this book.

I have prayed for you,
and the people you will share this book with.
If you are currently grieving in this season,
please know that you are not alone,
and that there is no timeline.
Don't be afraid to ask for help
and if you need someone to talk to,
do not hesitate to reach out to me.

I'd love to connect with you by email or social media.

Email: Josefina@loveoffering.co
Instagram: @LoveOffering

Made in the USA
San Bernardino, CA
02 July 2020